W9-BUR-354

Faithful and Courageous

Christians in Unsettling Times

_____

Bishop Mark S. Hanson

Augsburg Fortress

MINNEAPOLIS

FAITHFUL AND COURAGEOUS
Christians in Unsettling Times

Copyright © 2005 Augsburg Fortress. All rights reserved. Except for brief quotations in critical articles or reviews, no part of this book may be reproduced in any manner without prior written permission from the publisher. Write to: Permissions, Augsburg Fortress, Box 1209, Minneapolis, MN 55440.

Large-quantity purchases or custom editions of this book are available at a discount from the publisher. For more information, contact the sales department at Augsburg Fortress, Publishers, 1-800-328-4648, or write to: Sales Director, Augsburg Fortress, Publishers, P. O. Box 1209, Minneapolis, MN 55440-1209.

Scripture passages are from the New Revised Standard Version of the Bible, copyright © 1946, 1952, 1971, 1989 by the Division of Christian Education of the National Council of the Churches of Christ in the USA. Used by permission.

ISBN 0-8066-5182-2

Cover design by Diana Running; Cover photo © Design Exchange Co. Ltd./CORBIS.
Book design by Michelle L. N. Cook

The paper used in this publication meets the minimum requirements of American National Standard for Information Sciences—Permanence of Paper for Printed Library Materials, ANSI Z329.48-1984. ♾ ™

Manufactured in the U.S.A.

09   08   07   06   05   1   2   3   4   5   6   7   8   9   10

To Ione
woman of the prairie
whose faith embraces
grace and mystery
whose courage is resilient
whose love I cherish

Contents

see pg. 56, Resistance

Preface

We live in unsettling times marked by fear, uncertainty, anxiety, and distrust. People at all levels of society wrestle with deep life-challenging questions:

- Is there anyone in whom I can trust?
- How do I know what is true?
- What am I to do with my life?
- How can I live in this world as a person of faith?

A Lutheran pastor in Hawaii was disturbed by a campaign of bumper stickers that read "The Bible says it. I believe it. That settles it." The Lutheran pastor used a marker to alter the slogan to read, "That unsettles it."

When we read the Gospel accounts of Jesus, we recognize how unsettling were his words and deeds. He disrupted patterns of privilege, the rigidity of religious rulers, and the exclusion by pious people of those deemed unclean. As the good news of Jesus Christ spread and new people came to faith, their presence unsettled the ways of other faithful followers. To question whether Gentile converts needed to be circumcised had to be incredibly unsettling for Jewish Christians.

In such unsettling times as these, God calls us to be both faithful and courageous. We are faithful to God's call that sends us into the world as witnesses to the love and mercy and forgiveness of God. It takes courage to witness boldly. Paul said, "Keep alert, stand firm in your faith, be courageous, be strong." (1 Corinthians 15:13-14). Part of our bold witness in our perfectionist, hide-your-faults, deny-your-failures culture is to confess, "We are in bondage to sin and cannot free ourselves." In some contexts, it may take courage to act with humility. In other situations it will take courage to admonish one another, holding that person accountable. There are times it takes courage to admit we do not know with certainty what God is calling us to do.

God calls us—who often struggle with doubts and fears—and sends us out into the world, empowered by the Holy Spirit to be both faithful and courageous. We live out that faith and courage by:

- Trusting God's faithful promises;
- Pondering Jesus' probing questions;
- Obeying Jesus' unsettling commands;
- Discerning our way in the world.

This book is a sequel to *Faithful yet Changing: The Church in Challenging Times,* which identified seven marks of a faithful church. This present book speaks both to the life of the individual Christian living in the community of the church and to the communal expressions of the church—congregation, synod, and churchwide.

My thanks to Beth Lewis, CEO of Augsburg Fortress, Publishers, for asking me to write this book; her passion for the publishing ministry of this church is both courageous and inspiring. My thanks to Ron Klug, not only for his exceptional work as an editor but for his thoughtful reflections and contributions to the content. I also thank my colleagues who share in the leadership of the ELCA, whose living faith and courage are testimony to the work of the Holy Spirit.

My hope is that this book will encourage holy conversation about what it means to be faithful followers of Jesus in the body of Christ in these unsettling times. I hope it will be read by individuals who then will gather with other believers in new member classes, adult study, church councils, and other settings for lifelong learning in the church. May the Spirit bless our search for wisdom and our witness to the love of God in Christ Jesus our Lord.

Mark S. Hanson,
Presiding Bishop,
Evangelical Lutheran Church in America
President, Lutheran World Federation

1. Trusting God's Faithful Promises

People ask, "What has become of trust? Who is worthy of trust?" We live in a world marked by fear and distrust. People fear terrorism, crime, ecological disaster, illness, death, economic woes, an uncertain future. In 2004 we went through a contentious presidential campaign in which people on all sides of the political spectrum were said to have voted their fears. Scandals have rocked the corporate business sector and religious communities. Public leaders are seen as violating public trust. It has been a long time since I heard someone's word called "as good as gold." What words would we use today to describe someone who is absolutely trustworthy?

A society that finds few worthy of trust turns in upon itself. People distrust their leaders, disengage from institutions, distance themselves from communal life, and build barriers and walls to protect themselves from one another. When I became presiding bishop, a pastor said to me, "I think you are called to stand at the barriers we erect, that divide us from one another, and help us turn those walls into tables of conversation and reconciliation."

That image of turning walls that divide into tables that convene is helpful for all of us called into leadership in the church. Such leadership follows from what occurs at the Lord's table. There, Christ Jesus is our host, turning the walls of sinful and alienating lives into the Lord's table of forgiveness and reconciliation. Perhaps that is why I so often go back to Paul's words to the Corinthians: "So if anyone is in Christ, there is a new creation: everything old has passed away; see, everything has become new! All this is from God, who reconciled us to himself through Christ, and has given us the ministry of reconciliation" (2 Corinthians 5:17-18). Walls of fear become the arena for ministry grounded in faith.

Far too often, when fear becomes our orientation to the world, we either withdraw into isolation or resort to acts of aggression. Fear hardens lives and closes borders. Fear prevents us from being open to the radical newness of God's promises that call us to a life of faith.

Faith and courage prevent fear from becoming our defining reality. Faith calls us to see the world through the eyes of God's vision of *shalom*—a vision of the goodness of creation, of creation in harmony, of humanity interdependent.

Fear dares not acknowledge failures or expose weakness. Faith frees us to confess our bondage to sin, to acknowledge that we cannot free ourselves, and to accept the gift of forgiveness. Faith frees us by the power of the Holy Spirit to claim the promise that in Christ we are free to be bound and bound to be free. We are bound to God's promises through faith, bound to one another in love and the pursuit of peace with justice, bound to God's creation as stewards.

Fear causes us to be possessive of what we have, distrustful of others, and as Old Testament scholar Walter Brueggemann says, "downright anti-neighborly." Faith compels us to be engaged in the world, bearing witness to the signs of the inbreaking of God's reign of justice, mercy, and peace.

Fear turns us in upon ourselves, leaving us immobilized. Faith gives us courage to go out into the world. To terrified disciples the risen Christ appeared with a word of command and promise: "Peace be with you. As the Father has sent me, so I send you" (John 20:21). Right back out into the world that crucified Jesus, he sends his disciples. Yet not on their own: Jesus breathed on them saying, "Receive the Holy Spirit." We are sent in the power of the Holy Spirit with the promise of the good news of forgiveness.

Fear leaves us cynical toward the world. Faith compels us to take up our cross and follow Jesus, to respond to suffering in the world. Faith also calls us to rejoice, praising the Creator for the wonder, beauty, and mystery of life.

I will never forget my visit to Transfiguration Lutheran Church in the South Bronx in December of 2001. Pastor Heidi Neumark had preached at my installation service and invited me to preach in the congregation she was serving. It was only weeks after the 9/11 disaster. New York City residents were still in shock. The tremors of grief, depression, financial losses, and fear were being felt further and further out from the epicenter of the destruction. The challenges of affordable housing, available healthcare, quality schools, living wage jobs, and racism were great enough for the people of Transfiguration Lutheran and the Bronx *before* 9/11.

Yet on this first Sunday in Advent, the faithful gathered to praise Jesus and hear the good news proclaimed through Word and sacrament. Over thirty babies, children, adolescents, and adults were baptized that morning. Sitting in the front pew wrapped in bandages from burns suffered in the World Trade Center fires was the father of one who was baptized. In his face I saw the pain of his physical wounds and the joy of his faith and his delight as a parent. In the midst of almost immobilizing fear, faithful followers of Jesus were courageously and joyfully praising God and praying, "Come, Lord Jesus."

Into a context of fear and distrust God speaks faithful words of promise. In the biblical story we see many of the struggles of our own lives and our world mirrored. It can be comforting to know we are not unique; our situation is not unique. God's people throughout the ages have witnessed to God's faithfulness; their testimony calls us to be faithful and courageous.

Encountering God's Words of Promise

Where do we encounter God's faithful words of promise? We hear them in the Bible. Listen for a moment to just a few of these life-giving promises.

"The Advocate, the Holy Spirit, whom the Father will send in my name, will teach you everything, and remind you of all that I have said to you" (John 14:26).

"Believe on the Lord Jesus, and you will be saved, you and your household" (Acts 16:31).

"And if I go and prepare a place for you, I will come again and will take you to myself, so that where I am, there you may be also" (John 14:3).

"For by grace you have been saved through faith, and this is not your own doing; it is the gift of God" (Ephesians 2:8).

"I will build my church and the gates of Hades will not prevail against it" (Matthew 16:18).

"His divine power has given us everything needed for life and godliness, through the knowledge of him who called us by his own glory and goodness. Thus he has given us, through these things, his precious and very great promises, so that through them you may escape from the corruption that is in the world because of lust, and may become participants of the divine nature" (2 Peter 1:3-4).

"For I am convinced that neither death, nor life, nor angels, nor rulers, nor things present, nor things to come, nor powers, nor height, nor depth, nor anything else in all creation, will be able to separate us from the love of God in Christ Jesus our Lord" (Romans 8:38-39).

"God himself will be with them; he will wipe every tear from their eyes. Death will be no more; mourning and crying and pain will be no more" (Revelation 21:3-4).

So often it seems our fears close us off from hearing God's word of promise, from being open to God doing a new thing. Is it any wonder that God had to send messengers to announce "Do not be afraid"? The voice of the angels was startling enough, yet it paled in comparison to God's life-changing, life-giving, life-saving action. I often wonder who are the messengers God is sending to us and to whom are we being sent with the announcement "Do not be afraid!"

God sends messengers to create space for faith by inviting us not to be afraid. In that space God speaks a faithful word of promise, which is often a radically new word about what God is about to do for the sake of the creation and for God's people, each one of us.

In Isaiah 35 there is the promise of a homecoming from exile. To people who felt that God was not keeping promises or had abandoned them, God sent a messenger to say, "Be strong, do not fear!" (Isaiah 35:4). And then comes the beautiful description of homecoming, of the whole transformation of the creation, seen as a fulfillment of God's promises to bring God's people home: "Then the eyes of the blind shall be opened, and the ears of the deaf unstopped; then the lame shall leap like a deer, and the tongue of the speechless sing for joy. For waters shall break forth in the wilderness, and streams in the desert; the burning sand shall become a pool, and the thirsty ground springs of water."

In Luke's Christmas story the angel announces that God is about to fulfill the promise to be a living redeeming God by entering into the depths of human life, by becoming one with us and for us in Jesus Christ. But the shepherds were not ready to receive the radical newness of God's promise until they were first told, "Do not be afraid" (Luke 2:10).

The Easter encounters with the risen Christ too are preceded by an angel saying, "Do not be afraid; I know that you are looking for Jesus who was crucified. He is not here; for he has been raised" (Matthew 28:5-6).

Sometimes our familiarity with Scripture dampens the possibility that we will be as awe-struck as were those first hearers of the word of promise, but the biblical word always has the capacity to surprise us. We hear or read or remember a biblical text that we have heard many times before, and suddenly it breaks into new meaning. We hear it in a new way; we see it differently.

My father, Oscar Hanson, had been a vibrant personality, an eloquent preacher, a gifted writer. Through the ravages of Parkinson's disease he lost the ability to speak and write—and eventually to walk. Yet in the last few months and weeks of his life, we all knew that he was still communicating to us the love and grace of God. I remembered the promise in 2 Corinthians 2:14-16: "But thanks be to God, who in Christ, always leads us in trium-phal procession, and through us spreads in every place the fragrance that comes from knowing him. For we are the aroma of Christ to God among those who are being saved and among those who are perishing; to the one a fragrance from death to death, to the other, a fragrance from life to life." Unable to speak, yet through his loving embrace and whispered prayers, dad was spreading the aroma of Christ to us who struggled to make sense of his suffering. This text came alive to me in a new way, and I quoted it when I brought a greeting at his funeral.

Where do we speak and hear these promises of God?

God's word of promise is announced in worship, when the word of mercy and forgiveness is spoken and heard. Lutherans believe that when the living word of God is spoken, it in fact does that which it declares. The promise of forgiveness is not a promise that will be fulfilled in some future time but literally in the moment that the pastor says, "Almighty God, in his mercy, has given his Son to die for us and, for his sake, forgives us all our sins. As a called and ordained minister of the Church of Christ, and by his authority, I therefore declare to you the entire forgiveness of all your sins, in the name of the Father, and of the Son, and of the Holy Spirit."[1] By the power of God's Spirit we believe that in this very moment the promise is fulfilled and we are forgiven. I now have nothing in my past for which I have to atone before God, nothing in my future that I need to fear.

We hear God's word of promise in the sacraments. In Holy Baptism God is saying, "You are joined to Christ's death, raised to new life in Christ's body, bathed in my grace. I will love you steadfastly. I will forgive you mercifully. I will raise you up on the last day to eternal life. As a seal of that faithful promise, I give you the Holy Spirit.

As a sign of my faithfulness to you, I mark you with the cross of Christ forever." In that moment the final verdict on a life is already "leaked." God is saying, "Not guilty. You are innocent, not by virtue of what you have done or will do, but what God in Christ has done for you."

In the Lord's Supper we literally taste God's faithful promise in the bread and wine and hear it in the living word of Christ's promised presence and forgiveness: "This is my body given for you. This is my blood shed for you for the forgiveness of sins." In times of incredible stress, when God seems to have abandoned us and appears to be no longer faithful to God's promises, it is around the Lord's table that the faithful are gathered to receive the gift of God's faithfulness in Christ Jesus our Lord.

Our hearing God's faithful promises is not limited to one hour a week in the church building. We also hear God's words of promise in our homes and places of work and communities as we read the Scriptures, pray, and remind one another of God's promises. Luther called this the "mutual conversation and consolation" of brothers and sisters in Christ, and named it a means of grace.

Often it has been our children who have shown me the wonders of God's grace. When our children were young, there were days when I felt discouraged about my parenting, and the process of putting the children to bed didn't go very well—not even the bedtime prayers. I would come downstairs feeling bad. Even the next morning the discouraged feeling was still there. But then one of the children would come downstairs, see me sitting in a chair, and run and crawl up into my arms. In that loving embrace I was reminded of the promise of God's grace and forgiveness, which is new every morning. The day could then proceed not in guilt but in gratitude.

Entrusting Our Lives

Faith is entrusting one's whole life to God's faithful promises, the assurance that God will be faithful even when we are not. Faith is the result of God's faithfulness, a gift of the Holy Spirit.

Ione and I have a ritual in which we go to the country cemetery where her father is buried. First we go to his grave and share memories, shed tears, and say prayers. Then we each wander on our own, looking at tombstones.

One summer I saw one grave marker I had never noticed before. It said simply: "Hazel and Edward died in the faith of their Savior." They died not trusting in their own faith, but in the faith of their Savior. I take this to mean that it is Jesus' faithfulness that saves, not my faith. Jesus is both the source of my faith as well as the one in whom I have faith. Even my own faith is a sign of God's faithfulness, a gift of the Holy Spirit. The Book of Hebrews refers to Jesus as "the author and perfecter of our faith" (12:2).

When speaking on the mission of the church or leading a discussion on what it may mean to be followers of Jesus in a fearful world, I invite people to lay hands on someone else. Then we pray the prayer from the rite of the Affirmation of baptism: "Father in heaven, stir up in these women and men the gift of your Holy Spirit; confirm their faith. Guide their life, empower them in their serving, give them patience in suffering, and bring them to everlasting life." To which each person responds, "Amen."[2] It is a holy moment when we recognize that we cannot be faithful on our own. We are totally dependent on the power of the Holy Spirit and the community of faith.

God's Faithful Word of Promise

First of all, *God's promise clearly establishes my identity.* In part we are struggling as a church because we are not quite sure of our identity. Who are we really? What does it mean to be Christian? What does it mean that I have been claimed by grace and joined in the waters of baptism to the Triune God and to the community that bears Christ's name?

Once I heard on the radio the morning chapel service at St. Olaf College. The person preaching began, "Good morning. I am Tom. I'm a baptized believer in Jesus Christ, a Lutheran Christian. And I am your bus driver." Tom told his story of being a successful businessman who lost his career in the economic crisis in the 1980s, went into a personal depression, and came to renewed faith in the midst of this dark valley, a time when it must have seemed that God was not faithful to God's promises. He reached greater clarity about his identity as a baptized child of God but also about his vocation to drive St. Olaf and Carleton students back and forth between campuses.

When you introduce yourself to another person, what are the three things by which you most frequently identify yourself? How many of you say you are a Christian? I challenge people, "From now on boldly identify yourself as a Christian—like Tom the bus driver."

I often ride in taxicabs. I enjoy talking with the drivers, many of whom are recent immigrants. I ask about the country of their birth, whether they still have family there, the circumstances of their coming to the United States. We talk about faith. Often the driver states clearly, "I am a Muslim," "I am Christian," or "I am a Hindu." This leads to a discussion of whether they have found a community in which to practice their faith. I often leave with great respect for the clarity of their identity spoken and practiced.

It leaves me wondering why I and we as Christians often seem more hesitant to speak about who and whose we are, especially because we believe that our baptism into Christ's death and resurrection is the defining event of our lives.

When I taught confirmands, I told them, "When you are in the shower, draining the tank of all the hot water, recall how water was poured over you in baptism and say, 'I am baptized. I am chosen. I am a child of God. I belong to Jesus Christ.' Make the sign of the cross and recall how this day is begun in the promise of God's grace and forgiveness. You are sent into the world to live your faith through your many callings, as student, friend, family member, musician, athlete, but your identity has already been clearly given to you."

Second, *God's faithful promises create the community in which that identity was formed and has its grounding, the community of Christ's body, the church.* This means that my identity is both individual and communal, personal and corporate. Paul's image of us as members of the body of Christ—a living growing, changing organism—remains vivid and instructive: "For just as the body is one and has many members, and all the members of the body, though many, are one body, so it is with Christ" (1 Corinthians 12:12).

Third, *God's promises answer my need for meaning and purpose in life. This basic human need is as essential for a good life as the needs for food and shelter and loving relationships.* Some young adults are being criticized for not imitating the institutional loyalties their parents had for the church. In my discussions with young adults, what I hear them saying is, "I want to experience the presence of God in my life, and by virtue of the presence of God in my life, I want to make a difference in the world."

A group of college students exploring vocation visited with me. They were spending a week on a seminary campus, hearing lectures. I asked what they had learned. One young man responded with great enthusiasm, "I may not have this exactly right, but I learned that in Christ I am absolutely free—subject to no one—and at the same time, in Christ I am a servant to everyone. That is so cool!" He caught the freedom and responsibility that comes with the promise of new life in Christ.

Clinging to the Promise

Despite these gifts of identity, community, and purpose, there come times when all we can do is trust that God will be faithful to God's word of promise. A powerful Easter text for me is the words in Romans 8: "Nothing will be able to separate us from the love of God in Christ Jesus our Lord." Then Paul lists all the things that seek to separate us from God. God's love is always stronger even than death. The *what* of resurrection we leave to God, but *that* we will be raised to new life in Christ we must believe and proclaim.

When one of our sons was ordered by the court into a locked treatment facility for eighteen months for mental health and chemical dependency problems, we couldn't visit him for weeks until he had accommodated himself to the rules. Then Ione and I and our five other children went to visit him, bringing gifts and treats.

First, we had to go through a strict security check and had to be "wanded" before we walked through the metal detector. There we were— seven of us—spread out in cruciform shape, with outstretched arms and legs. The guard began to wand each one of us. Tears filled Ione's eyes, and she said, "Mark, he's making the sign of the cross with the wand."

In that moment of utter desperation about our son's future, all we could cling to was the promise that God spoke to our son at his baptism: "I love you steadfastly. I forgive you mercifully. You belong to me forever." We believed that God would be faithful even when we had no evidence that our son was being faithful to God. Now, ten years later our son has completed two years of post-high-school study and is finding stability in his life. He brings us great joy and delight.

When I taught confirmation, the class met one Saturday a month. In the morning we studied the Bible and catechism, and in the afternoon we discovered how that text was being lived out in our lives and in the lives of fellow members of the congregation. One Advent we visited a girl named Laurie, who would have been in the class except for a six-year battle with cancer. That December she was sent home from the hospital because there was nothing more the doctors could do for her. We went to her home and decorated the tree, sang carols, lit a candle, and read the Christmas Gospel, including the words: "Do not be afraid; for see—I am bringing you good news of great joy for all the people: to you is born this day in the city of David a Savior, who is the Messiah, the Lord" (Luke 2:10-11).

At our January class we called her mom and grandparents to join us as we stood on a bitter cold day at Laurie's grave, still mounded with dirt, the roses from the burial a week before frozen and black. We brought a candle, just as we had brought one to her home. We lit the candle and announced the promise: "Christ is risen for you, Laurie. Christ is risen indeed." And then we joined hands and sang:

> *Children of the heav'nly Father,*
> *Safely in his bosom gather;*
> *Nestling bird or star in heaven*
> *Such a refuge ne'er was given.*

Neither life nor death shall ever
From the Lord his children sever,
Unto them his grace he showeth,
And their sorrows all he knoweth.[3]

We were clinging to God's promise, even as we wept with Laurie's mother and grandparents. There are times when we need to speak God's faithful word of promise when we have little evidence that God is faithful.

In the Bible, God's people struggle with the question, "How do you live as people of faith when God seems absent?" One of my seminary professors said, "The existential question that is most pervasive in the Bible is not, how do we live in the presence of God? But, how do we live faithfully in the seeming absence of God?" In those moments I need to be surrounded by the community of believers that intercedes for me and announces God's merciful presence.

As a parish pastor, I often noted that people found church attendance most difficult after they had experienced wrenching losses—a divorce, trauma with a child, loss of a job, a death in the family. To such people I would say, "Come and be surrounded by the people who will sing the songs for you, pray for you, confess the creed on your behalf, who will be the community of confession and absolution when you feel totally isolated by your sorrow, your grief, your fear."

Some promises of God, like the promise of forgiveness proclaimed in worship, are fulfilled in the moment that we hear them. But for many of God's promises we need to wait for the fulfillment, to wait with patience and persistence, which does not come easily to us in a culture that wants everything right now. And while we wait, we need to discern whether God is waiting for us to be agents of God's gracious and merciful action.

While we live trusting and hoping in the promises of God that orient us to the future, we practice what Lutheran pastor "Joe" Bash called eschatological calisthenics.

For example, we hear God's promise in Revelation 21, "God himself will be with them; he will wipe away every tear from their eyes. Death will be no more; mourning and crying and pain will be no more." We do not just hold on to that promise only for the end of human history, but we exercise eschatological calisthenics in the present, as we go to those who mourn and wipe away their tears, as we go to the places where people are killing one another and begin to work for peace, declaring, "There will be no more death in this place." We are called and sent to live as signs of God's promised future.

On a recent trip to West Africa I experienced the power of such faithful witness. Both

Liberia and Sierra Leone have experienced the devastation of years of war—villages burned, limbs amputated, family members killed, homes fled, schools and hospitals destroyed. Huddled masses who gathered in St. Peter's Lutheran Church in Monrovia were brutally massacred. Some three hundred thousand Liberians fled to refugee camps within the country and in neighboring nations.

It is a context in which fear can understandably quell both faith and courage, yet each day of my trip we were met by women who were members of Women in Peacebuilding Network (WIPNET). They gather each morning in a public place for prayer. They plead for God's healing mercy as the nation rebuilds. Wherever they go, in their singing and dancing, their speaking and acts of compassion, they declare, "We will not see our husbands and children killed in war anymore." They dry the eyes of children orphaned; they keep hope alive that refugees might return home; they bear witness to the inbreaking of God's reign of justice, mercy, and peace.

Keeping Our Promises

By the power of the Spirit we trust God's faithful promises. In that faith we make promises to God and to one another. In the affirmation of baptism we ask, "Do you intend to continue in the covenant God made with you in Holy Baptism:

to live among God's faithful people,
to hear his Word and share in his supper,
to proclaim the good news of God in Christ through word and deed,
to serve all people, following the example of our Lord Jesus,
and to strive for justice and peace in all the earth?"[4]

These are indeed "big promises," difficult to fulfill. So the person responds, "I do, and I ask God to help me." We do not send the newly confirmed out on their own. They are immediately instructed to kneel to receive prayers and the laying on of hands to receive the Holy Spirit's presence and power.

Enlivened and strengthened by God's promises to us, we are called to make promises before God, to God, and to one another.

One is the promise parents and sponsors make at the baptism of children: to faithfully bring them to the services of God's house and provide for their instruction in the Christian faith. Another is the promise made at marriage. Ordination and installation take place in a community of promisers, who both make and receive promises.

In a society where promises are so often ignored or violated, how can we as the body of Christ strengthen and support one another in the promises we make? Can we hold one another accountable through words of admonition and affirmation, reminding one another of the promises made and at the same time affirming the assurance of God's forgiveness when promises are broken? If a child baptized in the faith is not seen in the church from the day of baptism on, who in the community of faith goes to the sponsors and parents to make sure their promises are being kept? If confirmands disappear from church within months of confirmation, who from the community of faith goes to remind them of their promises? How do we support those who make promises of faithfulness in marriage? What support and affirmation do we give pastors and the congregations that call them into ministry? Such calling one another to accountability reflects the congregation's intention to be faithful to the promises they made when asked, "And you, people of God, will you receive this messenger of Jesus Christ, sent by God to serve God's people with the Gospel of hope and salvation? Will you regard *him/her* as a servant of Christ and a steward of the mysteries of God?" and they answer, "We will." And again, "Will you pray for *him/her,* help and honor *him/her* for *his/her* work's sake, and in all things strive to live together in the peace and unity of Christ?" and they answer, "We will." [5]

In addition to supporting individual promise-makers, how do we as citizens and as the church call public officials or corporate officers to account for the promises they have made to their constituents?

One way is through what is known as congregation-based organizing. In St. Paul, Minnesota, church members observed the increased detention of immigrants for lack of documentation, and even their arrest and deportation. When one thousand people of faith called the Immigration and Naturalization Services to insist that those detained have access to telephone, translation, and legal services, the director began to make changes and agreed to meet in the future with representatives of the religious community. When his promises were made and monitored publicly, the behavior of government changed.

Are we not called to pray for, to affirm and admonish one another as we seek to be faithful to the promises we make?

Being faithful is about making and keeping promises. God is faithful to us by promising life, healing, and salvation for the world. Through the power of the Holy Spirit we entrust our lives to those promises of God. And in the power of the Spirit we make promises to God and one another.

We support one another in keeping those promises, and we are enabled to hold to the promises because we know that when we fail, we are still held in the promises of God's love and forgiveness.

Questions for Reflection and Discussion

1. Do you agree that we live in a world marked by fear and distrust? How do you experience that in your life?

2. Reread the biblical promises on pp. 14-15. What does each one mean for your life?

3. What are some promises of God that mean the most to you?

4. In what areas of your life do you most need to hear God's word, "Do not be afraid"? In what areas of your congregation's life?

5. Where in the worship service do you hear God's word of promise? Where do you hear it outside the church building?

6. Can you identify a time in your life when all you had to cling to was a promise of God? What happened?

7. What do you understand by the term "eschatological calisthenics"? How might you be practicing it?

8. What are some promises you have made? How might your congregation help members keep the promises they make to God or to one another?

9. How might we as citizens or as a church call to account government, corporate, or religious leaders?

10. What did you find most interesting or helpful in this chapter?

11. What questions do you have as a result of studying this chapter?

In your Bible reading, be alert for promises of God. Write them in your journal. Memorize them. Speak them to another person.

2. Pondering Jesus' Probing Questions

"Jesus is the answer." That statement of faith is announced on bumper stickers, over airwaves, and from pulpits. Although its simplicity may be offensive to some, its clarity is admirable to many.

Yes, Jesus is God's answer to human sinfulness: "the lamb of God who takes away the sin of the world" (John 1:29). Jesus is God's response to human alienation: "In Christ God was reconciling the world to himself" (2 Corinthians. 5:19). Jesus is God's pursuit of the lost and forsaken, declaring, "I am the way, and the truth, and the life" (John 14:6). The crucified and risen Christ is God's resounding *no* to the finality of death and *yes* to new life in Christ and the way of the cross. Many, if not most, of the stories about Jesus are of his being the answer to our longings for hope and healing, for forgiveness and faith.

Jesus the Questioner

Often overlooked in the Gospel stories is Jesus the questioner. Jesus had the audacity to ask questions when one might have expected him to be silent or to offer words of comfort or conviction.

Jesus questions Mary, who is in a parent's panic over her lost child: "Why were you searching for me? Did you not know that I must be in my Father's house?" (Luke 2:49).

Jesus' question challenges religious leaders: "Is it lawful to cure people on the sabbath, or not?" (Luke 14:3).

Even his own disciples are not spared Jesus' probing questions: "Who do people say that I am? But who do you say that I am?" (Mark 8:27-29). The risen Christ relentlessly questioned Peter: "Do you love me more than these?" "Do you love me?" "Do you love me?" (John 21:15-17).

Not even God is exempt from Jesus' questioning. I take great comfort that in his dying breath Jesus asked, "My God, my God, why have you forsaken me?" (Mark 15:33). If it was all right for Jesus to cry out in the face of God's seeming absence, then am I not free to ask the same question?

Even after his ascension, Jesus inquired of the apostle Paul: "Saul, Saul, why do you persecute me?" (Acts 9:4).

Jesus the questioner invites us to experience the depth of God's grace and mercy.

As we read the probing questions of Jesus, they are asking us to reassess our lives as well as his. For example, in our age of "family values"

Jesus asks, "Who is my father and mother, my brother and sister?" He answers, "Those who do God's will," and thereby asks us to reevaluate our primary relationships (Mark 3:33-35).

"Who do people say that I am?" Jesus asks. "Who do you say that I am?" That may be the most provocative question for every one of us, because the Bible doesn't answer that in any single or simple way. Jesus continues to be seen as savior, liberator, healer, teacher, friend, son of God. According to the Bible Jesus is all of these—and more. As faithful witnesses we should always be ready to answer the question, "Who is Jesus for you?"

A pastor was leaving a congregation after twelve years of ministry there. For his farewell sermon he decided to abandon the prescribed Bible texts and to preach personally from the heart about who Jesus is for him. As people were saying goodbye at the church door, one woman was particularly tearful. He thought, *She's upset about my leaving.* When he asked her what was the matter, she replied, "Why did you take so long to tell us?"

The Value of Questions

Trusting God's faithful promises does not mean that we have no doubts, no questions. It is just the opposite. God's promise of faithfulness gives us the freedom to express our doubts, to raise our questions, to engage in the human quest to discover meaning for our lives.

I wish we could spend more time as people of faith pondering the probing questions Jesus asks of us. Jesus' questions often invited his hearers to critical reflection on their lives, leading them to repentance. Jesus' questions opened those questioned to see differently the presence and promises of God. Jesus' questions were sometimes accusatory, sometimes a gracious invitation to conversation and conversion.

What if we took a break from dealing with our most pressing issues to respond to Jesus' probing questions of us? Questions like:

"Why do you call me 'Lord, Lord,' and do not do what I tell you?" (Luke 6:46).

"Why do you see the speck in your neighbor's eye but do not notice the log in your own eye?" (Luke 6:41).

"Where is your faith?" (Luke 8:25).

"You know how to interpret the appearance of earth and sky, but why do you not know how to interpret the present time?" (Luke 12:56).

"What do you want me to do for you?" (Luke 18:41).

"Why are you frightened, and why do doubts arise in your hearts?" (Luke 24:38).

Over and over in the Small Catechism Luther raises the question, "What does this mean?" That question should be part of the daily and weekly vocabulary for people of faith. What do God's faithful promises mean for me, for us? What do God's commands mean for me, for us? What does stewardship of the earth mean for us and for others? What does this action of our government mean for us and for others in the world? What do the policies of transnational corporations mean for us and for others?

On a retreat I found a journal entry left by a previous retreatant: "I came here seeking answers to some very difficult questions. After this time of prayer and Scripture, I now realize that it is not the answers one gives but the questions with which one lives that give evidence of faith."

As I travel throughout this church and the world, I value the opportunity to listen and seek to respond to questions. Questions so often reveal our longing for greater clarity in a complex world and conflicted church. Our willingness to ponder probing questions—Jesus' and ours—can contribute to the strength of our faithfulness and courage in a fearful world.

Questions invite us to contemplate the mystery of being human, the complexity of relationships, and the wonder of God's grace. The Lutheran theologian Joseph Sittler wrote: "What I am appealing for is an understanding of grace that has the magnitude of the Holy Trinity. The grace of God is not simply a holy hypodermic whereby my sins are forgiven. It is the whole giftedness of life, the wonder of life, which causes me to ask questions that transcend the moment."[1]

It has been people who live on farms and in rural communities who have often been my mentors when it comes to experiencing God's grace. I was awakened in the middle of the night to observe lambing on the Schwartz farm. Joanne became midwife when the labor became difficult. The lambs that were most fragile were wrapped in blankets and brought into the kitchen for warmth and care. As Joanne wearily nurtured those lambs, marveling in the gift of life, she wondered aloud why so often we take life for granted and seem almost callous to the suffering of those people who struggle daily to experience dignity and hope.

Questions can become the occasion for deepening faith and growing wisdom. A songwriter was composing a musical on Jesus' Sermon on the Mount. He came into my office asking what I thought Jesus meant when he said, "For I tell you, unless your righteousness exceeds that of the scribes and Pharisees, you will never enter the kingdom of heaven" (Matthew 5:20).

Rather than giving an off-the-cuff answer, I suggested we explore the verse together. So we began to meet regularly—reading the Bible, talking about Martin Luther's understanding of the righteousness of God, and contemplating how such a complex concept might be captured in a musical. It was amazing what a question set in motion.

Lively questions can enrich the community of believers as we invite people to Christ and work together for justice and peace. Before the first anniversary of 9/11, I was invited to the White House with a group of interfaith leaders to share with President Bush reflections on the significance of 9/11 and to pray. I received the invitation while speaking to a group of pastors in Ohio. So I asked them, if you were going to speak with the President about the significance of 9/11, what would you say?

A pastor in her first call said she would share the story of where she was on 9/11. She was visiting a couple who had gone to the hospital in labor about to deliver their first child. The labor was difficult and drawn out. She stayed with the couple and during interludes between contractions they began to watch on television the unfolding events of that tragic day.

Just as the second tower of the World Trade Center crashed to the ground, the baby came through the birth canal. The pastor said, "I would share that story with the president and then I would add, 'Mr. President, please do not ever forget that in the midst of death and destruction, God has promised to labor to bring forth life.'" The next day I shared that story with President Bush. My clear question— what would you say?—provided occasion for a pastor's powerful witness to God's grace and mercy born out of a life experience.

Truth-Discerning Communities

Faith seeks understanding. We are questioners; we are also those questioned. At times I wonder if our multi-tasking, frenetic lives are not a means of avoiding searching questions. Someone said to me, "I am living at such a ridiculous pace that it seems I must eat tomorrow's meal today in order to give me strength for yesterday's work."

Where can I go to get help with the questions life asks of me, especially those that keep me awake in the night? I can't find the answers alone. I need a community that helps me discern the truth among the myriad conflicting ideas and views with which I am bombarded daily. Our congregations can be such truth-discerning communities.

In my last parish ministry I began to teach the adult class for new members by asking those gathered, "What questions about faith and life are you asking?" We would write those questions on the board, and they would shape our time together for six weeks. This became a rich way to explore the faith, and along the way I would weave in the key doctrines of the Christian faith.

As a teacher of confirmation I felt I had failed if a confirmand was ready to affirm his or her baptism but had no questions. A week or two before their confirmation, each one came to see me with his or her parents. I asked them to write out the meaning of some words that are central to the vocabulary of faith, and I would ask them to write their own statement of faith. I would add, "Please tell me at least two questions that you're now asking *because* you've been in confirmation class, questions for which you still have no answers." They always raised thoughtful, provocative questions—questions such as, "Do I have to accept the creation story in Genesis as literal fact to be a Christian?" "Will people of other faiths be saved?" "Where is hell anyway?" "Why do classmates from school accept me when we are in church but ignore me at school?" This conversation around students' questions became a model for the parents sitting in the room, who may have been uneasy asking questions.

One summer in the parish I told people I was willing to set aside the lectionary texts. I asked, "What are some themes or biblical texts that you would like me to address?" The most common questions were around the theme: "Where is God in my suffering? Why does God permit evil and suffering?" These questions became occasions for lively discussion after tragedies in the nation or individual lives.

In our congregations, do we welcome questions or regard them as signs of weak faith? If questions are discouraged, is it any wonder young adults often leave the church when they are asking questions of identity, authority, and loyalty? Where in the life of our congregation are questions encouraged? When do we take time with our questions? If there is never time or space for questions, or if we're afraid that we will sound ignorant or foolish, we limit our growth as Christians.

Questions can be the openings to wisdom. Wisdom, according to my colleague Jonathan Strandjord, comes in two ordinary flavors. "First of all, there is the wisdom which serves desire. I want something, so I learn how to make or otherwise get hold of it." A second and contrary kind of wisdom is the wisdom that reduces craving, "which aims to replace hot desire with cool detachment." According to Dr. Strandjord, neither of these two kinds of wisdom are wrong, but there is a third: the wisdom that belongs to faith and makes us "other-wise." "Being other-wise is a fundamental orientation, a basic posture, an over-arching purpose."

Being other-wise takes us out of ourselves and places us before our neighbor. "There we are both free and called to be *thoughtful*. . . . It is deep thought for the sake of the other. It is mindful generosity." [7]

For many of the questions of our time, the answers are complex. We need to resist the temptation to settle for easy, simplistic answers, even though they sound self-assured. We must live with the humility that says, "I may be wrong." We must, as the German poet Rilke wrote, learn to love the questions.

How can we read Jesus' encounters in the Gospels, the struggles of the early Christians in Acts, the controversies in the epistles, the spiritual warfare in the Book of Revelation, and conclude that living in God's promises in today's world will be free of tensions and conflicts? I'm more concerned about a church—congregation, synod, or denomination—that seems to be tension-free than one that is actively engaged in questions that create tensions and even conflict. The challenge is to make sure that the questions with which we are struggling are for the sake of the gospel, faith, and the life of the world. The challenge is to remain healthy as individuals and the church as we confront unsettling questions and often profound disagreements.

Listening and Telling

In a truth-discerning community we need to be a body of listeners who listen not only to those in positions of authority and power, but those at the margins of our society. In *Life Together* Dietrich Bonhoeffer wrote: "The *first* service one owes to others in the community involves listening to them. Just as our love for God begins with listening to God's Word, the beginning of love for other Christians is learning to listen to them. God's love for us is shown by the fact that God not only gives us God's Word but also lends us God's ear. We do God's work for our brothers and sisters when we learn to listen to them."[3]

After listening, we may be better able to communicate truth to others. The Rev. John H. Thomas, general minister and president of the United Church of Christ, has said that among the leaders needed by the church today are prophets or truth tellers. "We live in a culture rampant with self-deception, where the temptations to deceive ourselves about the most fundamental realities facing our lives is encouraged in the highest offices, and, sadly in many pulpits. Prophets are truth tellers, but perhaps even more important, they discern truth for and within the community of faith."[4]

At the same time as God's people need pastors and theologians who proclaim truth and help the church discern truth, we also can benefit from what someone has called the "prophethood of all believers." To deal with the complex issues of our time, we also receive valuable insights from the laity who work in medicine and law, in business and economics, in agriculture and conservation, in social work and community development, in journalism and broadcasting, in politics and government, in education and job training, in factories and restaurants, and those who live with the reality of poverty and violence.

As truth-tellers in our congregations we remember that Martin Luther described Christians as being at the same time saints and sinners. Former ELCA presiding bishop H. George Anderson has written: "And with this understanding we may, as a church, be less inclined to speak with ultimate authority for God on all issues. Instead, we encourage study and mutual conversation on complex issues, realizing that our own self-interest may cloud our perceptions. We recognize that not all truth may be on our side. We are not yet God, so our pronouncements must always be examined for self-interest and self-righteousness. But we are free to do that because we believe that our salvation does not depend on our being right."[5]

The world is not divided between good people and bad people; but the line between good and evil runs through the heart of each of us. This, as Dr. Anderson has said, "should help in trying to promote a climate of moral deliberation. It ought to provide a check on my own position in which I say, 'Wait a minute. I really do need to hear what these other people are saying.' There's likely to be more self-interest in what I say than I'm willing to admit. I always learn from the voice of the other."[6]

We can live with the questions only because of the promises. Because God is faithful to us, we are free to ask questions, knowing that we are not saved by having all the right answers. If we sometimes get it wrong, we have the assurance of God's grace and forgiveness. This assurance gives us the faith and courage both to hear and speak truth to one another for our mutual growth in wisdom and the life of faith. "Speaking the truth in love, we must grow up in every way into him who is the head, into Christ, from whom the whole body, joined and knit together by every ligament with which it is equipped, as each part is working properly, promotes the body's growth in building itself up in love" (Ephesians 4:15-16).

Questions for Reflection and Discussion

1. To what extent is your congregation a safe place to ask questions? Where in the life of your congregation are questions encouraged?

2. How would you respond to each of the biblical questions on p. 38?

3. What are some questions you would like an opportunity to ask? What are some Bible texts that you would like to learn more about?

4. What would it mean for you to become more "other-wise"?

5. How do you respond to the statement, "I am more concerned about a church . . . that seems to be tension-free than one that is actively engaged in questions that create tensions and even conflict"?

6. How would you rate your own ability as a listener? Who are the people in your life who best listen to you? Where in the life of your congregation does good listening occur?

7. Whom do you identify as the prophets or truth-tellers in your congregation, your synod, the ELCA, or your community? What makes that person a prophet or truth-teller for you?

8. What did you find most interesting or helpful in this chapter?

9. What questions do you have as a result of studying this chapter?

In your Bible reading, be alert to the questions expressed. Use them as occasions for reflection, journaling, and prayer.

3. Obeying Jesus' Unsettling Commands

"If you love me," Jesus said, **"you will keep** my commandments" (John 14:15).

"Everyone then who hears these words of mind and acts on them will be like a wise man who built his house on rock" (Matthew 7:24).

"All authority on heaven and earth has been given to me. Go therefore and make disciples of all nations, baptizing them in the name of the Father and of the Son and of the Holy Spirit, and teaching them to obey everything that I have commanded you" (Matthew 28:18-20).

When asked which was the greatest commandment, Jesus answered directly, "Love the Lord your God with all your heart and soul and mind." This is the first commandment, and everything else is based on it, including the second commandment, "Love your neighbor as yourself." Our obedience to the commands of God grows out of our love for God and our worship of God.

In his book *Loving Jesus*, Mark Allan Powell declares, "We exist as a church to worship God and love Jesus, and one way that we worship God and love Jesus is by living the way that God wants us to live and doing the work that Jesus would have us do."[1]

God's Word of Command

How can we read the Bible and not hear God's word of expectation and command? The law reveals God's will for us and our need for repentance and forgiveness. We hear the word of God as both gospel and law, promise and command. In this tension between law and gospel, God's intentions for human life and behavior still stand. Because we are still both saints and sinners, the commands reveal our brokenness and our need of grace. For these two reasons we don't just set the commandments aside. God's gracious concern for life, health, and good order in the community is also present in the law.

In his book *The Christian's Calling in the World* Mark Kolden writes: "Luther saw from the Bible that good works are commanded by God, so they are not optional. But what makes them good is not that they are done for God but that they serve people in need. Luther said, 'A good work is good for one's neighbor.' Good works are not for eternal life but for this life, here and now. God commands them because God loves this world and wants to get it loved through our good works."[2]

God's intentions for humanity, as expressed for example in the Ten Commandments, are not burdens or restrictions but words of freedom, gifts of God's love and mercy. Before giving the commandments, God acted in a saving way by freeing the people of Israel from bondage. In the wilderness, when they were longing to return to bondage, God gave them the Ten Commandments, saying in effect, "If you live according to them, you will continue to experience the freedom that I gave you." God's commands are about freedom, about living in the power of God's Spirit. Freedom is expressed in protecting one another's lives and property, in honoring elders and parents, in keeping Sabbath. Luther captured this positive dimension in his explanations to the commandments in the Small Catechism. For example, in explaining the Fifth Commandment, "You shall not murder," he says, "We are to fear and love God, so that we neither endanger nor harm the lives of our neighbors, but instead help and support them in all of life's needs."[3]

Like the people of Israel in Egypt, we are in bondage—to sin. God's word of forgiveness frees us to live a new life in accordance with God's will. In the community of faith we are led by God's word as we hear it in the Bible and from our brothers and sisters, who help us discern what the words of God mean for us in the specific situations of our lives.

While recognizing the ongoing authority of God's law, we acknowledge both *conflict* and *ambivalence* about the commands. We are dual creatures, both sinner and saint. The old sinful nature still clings to us, so a part of us says, "Don't tell me what to do!" The new self that God creates in us day by day says, "I rejoice to do your will, O Lord" (Psalm 40:8).

What causes us to resist the commandments?

- resentment over more burdens in an already burdened life
- reluctance to induce guilt in ourselves or others
- resistance to authority
- recognition that obedience is costly to us.

Resentment Over Burdens
We live under the weight of expectations of others and ourselves. If we hear the commands of Jesus only as additional burdens on already overloaded lives, they may prevent us from hearing the word of grace and lead us only to despair. We want to do the will of God, but feel we cannot.

Reluctance to Induce Guilt
We may avoid speaking or thinking about the commandments in Scripture because we are wary of producing guilt—in ourselves or others. Although some have maintained that guilt is always a bad

thing, psychologist Evelyn Eaton Whitehead and religious historian James D. Whitehead point out the benefits of guilt: "Guilt reminds us of the shape of our best self; alerts us to discrepancies between ideals and behavior; defends the commitments and value-choices through which we give meaning to our life; it supports our sense of *personal integrity*."[4]

Guilt has value when it leads us to repentance, to turning back toward God, the divine word of forgiveness, and God's will for our lives. Because of sin—our curved-in-upon-self living—we cannot save ourselves or make our lives whole. To repent is to shout out, "I can't! We can't!" To repent is to put on the brakes and come to a full stop. To repent is to confess that the path of our lives has come to a dead end.

In the small South Dakota town where my dad was raised the railroad line came to an end. When a train arrived, the town whistle blew. Men went to the rail yard, inserted long poles into a round platform, and together they turned the locomotive around so it could travel in the right direction.

What a marvelous image of repentance! The Spirit, through the gospel, turns our dead-end lives from sin toward God's forgiveness in Christ Jesus. Warning signs are given so we might be turned toward God's promised future for ourselves and for others. When the Spirit turns us, we not only receive God's promised future in faith but also respond to others with generosity and justice, fruits worthy of repentance.

Just as it took a community to turn the locomotive so it often takes a community to heed the warning signs that we are on a self-destructive course as individuals, as a human race. A family intervenes with a chemically dependent loved one, giving clear examples of his or her dead-end behavior. The assurance of their love and the examples of DUIs, job loss, and health problems are followed by the clear statement: "You cannot go on living this way. We want you to get help, to go to treatment."

Jesus is God's loving intervention for the sake of the healing of the world in bondage to sin. God's commands are often a call to repent, to be turned toward life in God's saving grace in Christ Jesus. Receiving God's grace in Christ through faith turns us from death to life and transforms us.

When Ione and the children and I were in family therapy, a counselor, a Roman Catholic layperson, said to me: "You spend a lot of time dwelling on what you could have or wish you would have done differently. Who speaks God's word of forgiveness to you, Mark? And when it's spoken, do you believe it?" His admonition made me recognize that bearing the burdens of parenting had caused me not to trust the very word of forgiveness I was announcing to others.

Resistance to Authority

For some people any talk about commands implies a commander, and that feels to them like a hierarchical or military or monarchical picture of God. However, if we say with the early Christians, "Jesus is Lord," there is an element of accountability in my relationship with God. When the early Christians said "Jesus is Lord," they meant that Caesar was not Lord, and that was a radical act. For German Christians in the 1930s, "Jesus is Lord" meant Hitler is not Lord. For us too it means no human power is Lord, and that means I am not the center of the universe, nor are any of the leaders or institutions that demand my allegiance. Though we might be tempted to make gods of other things or human beings or ourselves, there is one God and one Lord whom we worship. Some part of me resists that, but if I want to reduce God only to a friend or someone who assists me in doing my will, we are missing the radical call to discipleship.

Perhaps we can learn from Luther's way of describing the paradox of obedience in "The Freedom of the Christian": "A Christian is a perfectly free Lord of all, subject to none. A Christian is a perfectly dutiful servant of all, subject to all."[5]

In Hebrew, the word *obey* is closely related to the word for listen. We respond to what we hear from a loving God, who expresses a desire, an intention for our relationship. Obedience, then, occurs in a relationship with a loving God, who has great expectations for those whom God loves.

It is Jesus who commands us. The Bible speaks of us as being in Christ and of Christ being in us. By faith we participate in the life of Christ. Paul encourages us to "put on the Lord Jesus Christ" (Romans 13:14). We can say with Paul, "It is no longer I who live, but it is Christ who lives in me" (Galatians 2:20). In a profound sense it is Christ in us who obeys Christ's commands. We can say with the psalmist: "I delight to do your will, O my God" (Psalm 40:8).

The Cost of Obedience

Perhaps the deepest reason we resist talk about commands is that we fear the cost of obedience. We sense that to heed God's commands may lead to lives of costly discipleship. The price of following Jesus is that we will be called to live the way of the cross, which ultimately cost Jesus his life. Jesus' unsettling commands call for a radical change of life: "Pray for your enemies. Sell all that you have and give to the poor. Leave all you have and follow me."

Darrell Jodock of Gustavus Adolphus College in St. Peter, Minnesota, has written that one impediment to our discipleship in the world is too "pedestrian" a delineation of Christian identity. "A pedestrian view expects no more of Christians than conventional morality. The chief goal of conventional morality is to avoid transgression: *not* being a bigot, *not* harming anyone else physically, *not* cheating, and the like. If that's all that is expected, then Christian faith seems to many in our society quite superfluous. They rightly point out that one does not need to be religious to be moral in this conventional way. But Christians are called to a more radical morality—one of turning the other cheek, of going the second mile, of seeking justice even at one's own expense, of self-discipline for the sake of the other, of seeking peace rather than pursuing vengeance. Without some vision of the radicality of the Christian ethic, there can be no authentic discipleship."[6]

Mark Powell has pointed out that in the Gospels Jesus never asked if he could come into someone's heart. Jesus is always inviting us to come and live in him. If we invite Jesus into our life, we are more likely to want to take Jesus where we want him to go. When we live in Christ, Jesus will often take us where we do not want to go. Jesus never said, "May I come and follow you?" but "Are you ready to come and follow me?" When we take up our cross to follow Jesus, we may be led to costly discipleship or even death.

In his book *Witnessing for Peace* Munib Younan, Bishop of Jerusalem in the Evangelical

Lutheran Church of Jordan and the Holy Land, Jerusalem, recalls how Harold Fisher, a sixty-year-old German doctor, was killed by an Israeli helicopter gunship, while seeking to minister to Palestinian people under attack by the Israelis. At his funeral, attended by Dr. Fisher's wife and children, Bishop Younan referred to the doctor as a "martyr for peace."

Afterward, reporters asked the bishop, "Why did you refer to Dr. Fisher as a martyr? Doesn't one have to die fighting to be a martyr?"

Bishop Younan comments: "I was once again reminded that the church needs a theology of *martyria*. It's a concept misunderstood, misused, and even missing from the vocabularies of many Christians. What does it mean to be a martyr? In a simple sense, it means no more than to be a witness. That's how it is translated. It means a life of witnessing in word, and also in deed. That's why someone like Harold Fisher was such a good witness. His whole life expressed his faith—his calling as a doctor, his constant love and care for those in need, his attitude of humble service. Dr. Fisher did not hesitate to speak of his faith, but what is more important, he lived it. So he witnessed in word and deed. The third component is suffering. *Martyria* is expressed when one's faith makes one vulnerable to the suffering of this world. It means exposing oneself, risking one's life for the other, as Dr. Fisher did."[7]

We must be cautious in speaking of a following that leads to death. Martyrdom can be an expression of politicized fundamentalism that creates death and destruction rather than life. Yet there is a proper place for costly witness or *martyria*. I remember the times that Bishop Younan has called me in a moment of crisis for the Palestinian people and said, "Mark, this is the time for faithful witness."

One Easter evening Bishop Younan was describing the shooting going on in the streets of Ramallah and how he had to make the decision that three of the Lutheran congregations could not hold worship on Easter morning because it would put people at risk going through the checkpoints. He asked, "Mark, are the people of the ELCA praying for peace?" I assured him that we were. Then he asked, "Are the people of the ELCA ready to be faithful witnesses for the sake of peace and justice in the Middle East?" I did not respond, because I did not know how many of us were willing to experience the costly side of obedience.

Communities of Ethical Discernment

Many of the commands of Jesus are clear to us. We understand—perhaps only too well—what they expect of us. But because we live in a time that presents us with new challenges, new moral questions unknown to the biblical writers, God's commands as we learn them from the Bible and in the church need to be interpreted in a community of discernment.

Lutheran pastor and seminary professor Lisa E. Dahill explains what Christians mean by discernment: "the deeply prayerful capacity to look to God for direction, to keep our eyes on Jesus Christ and his leading daily—especially in times of complexity, crisis, and fear. When anxieties rise, we may be tempted to do something—*anything* to resolve the situation. Or we can become paralyzed and unable to act at all. In either case it's easy to lose sight of the one whose ways are often hidden and unexpected, whose presence can take us by surprise. This is no clear or simple task but a complex spiritual discipline requiring years of practice in attending to God."[8]

Practicing discernment has never been easy for Christians, but it is perhaps even more difficult in our day, when society provides few absolute guidelines and when new ethical dilemmas confront us. Joseph Sittler, writing about the new ethical questions raised by contemporary medical advances, wrote: "In each succeeding generation ethical issues demand ever deeper insight. Our parents knew as well as we that the Christian obligation is to hear the will of God and do it. In most instances, they could find laws, biblical precedents, comparable instances, and analogies whereby to guide their steps. They could ask with a certain admirable directness, 'What does the Word of God teach concerning these matters?' We must ask the same question, but we cannot with equal clarity discern a guiding counsel for many problems of our time. Neither Scripture nor the body of Christian tradition can be transposed with adequate clarity into the tangled web of contemporary life. Fresh approaches are needed."[9]

Concerning the overwhelming number of needs and questions facing our world and this church, I am grateful for the insight of one Lutheran pastor who said, "We cannot respond to all the questions at the same time. Yet sometimes it seems we lack a way to determine which require our most immediate response. We need to learn as a church how to engage in 'ethical triaging.'" (In a medical situation, triaging involves dealing with the most urgent or important cases first.) How do we as individuals, congregations, communities, and a church choose which issues require our most immediate response?

Ethical triaging involves prayer and the study of the Bible. It calls for an assessment of the gifts, insights, and resources we bring. It leads us to ask with whom we might join in our response. Ethical triaging implies a willingness to make difficult decisions, recognizing that as individuals and a church, we cannot respond to every need and issue. We need to trust that sometimes others will act on our behalf, or we may need to let some pressing problem wait for our response.

As Lutherans we affirm the authority of the Bible as the norm for our faith and life, but this does not absolve us from the responsibility of discerning what the Bible says to our lives. We need much more conversation about how to do that, but we have some agreed upon principles for interpreting the Bible today, among them:

- We do not isolate individual passages, but read them in the context of the whole of the Bible.
- We seek to understand the Bible in its historical context even as we seek to discern its meaning in our context.
- We recognize that some parts of the Bible are more important than others—those that lead us to Christ.
- We interpret the Bible in the light of the Bible.
- We remember that the Bible is both law and gospel, demand and promise.

Mark Powell has written: "Virtually all Christian sects and individuals will grant that some prescriptions and proscriptions of Scripture are no longer relevant or applicable to Christians in the world today. . . . The challenge . . . is to recognize that questions of permanent or continuing relevance must be raised and yet to find a way of engaging those questions with a sub-missive integrity that respects the authority of Scripture over its interpreters. We cannot simply insist on universal and permanent applicability of all scriptural mandates, but we must avoid the temptation of deciding that directives no longer apply to us simply because they are no longer in sync with the shifting values of the age."[10]

How do congregations become communities of ethical discernment and moral formation? The Bible and the commands of Jesus shape how we live as moral creatures. This does not mean that we will always be in agreement regarding what is the moral and just response to complex questions. For the sake of harmony it is tempting for congregations to avoid struggling with deeply held convictions that reveal members are not of one mind, even as they share one faith, one Spirit, one baptism.

It is also easy to mirror our argumentative culture. Following that method, we ask those who hold polar opposite positions to debate them. Then we write a resolution for a congregational meeting or synod assembly. Normally, after a fairly brief and often intense debate, we ask people to vote. The prevailing side is deemed to have won the argument.

This method can become an increasing hindrance to a congregation becoming a community of moral deliberation. In one congregation I served, we created a task force on moral deliberation. The ten members reflected the diversity of the congregation. They spent one entire year studying what it means to engage in moral deliberation as a community of faith. They examined rules for moral discourse and tried various models. Only after a year of exploring the challenging topic were they ready to mentor the congregation.

The process did not deny the authority of the Bible or disregard God's commands. In fact, because of attention to both the Christian tradition and our context, our process of moral discernment became an example of the interrelatedness between obedience and discernment.

Lisa E. Dahill stresses our need for communities of discernment: "Since we easily deceive ourselves, we need to open our hearts to others' gaze. Very often the sins from which God is most eager to redeem us are ones we are quite blind to on our own.

"So we need trusted friends in Christ to help us distinguish inner voices that harm us or others from places where God is longing to invite us into greater freedom and love. Whether in spiritual direction, in 12-step programs, or in ongoing faith-sharing with close companions, we each need places where we learn to speak and hear and receive the living truth of Christ."[11]

Conscience Bound by the Word of God

Lutherans respect the conscience bound by the word of God. We follow Luther who had the faithfulness and courage to stand against both the religious community and the state, declaring, "My conscience is captive to the word of God. I cannot and I will not retract anything, since it is neither safe nor right to go against conscience."[12]

Timothy Wengert comments: "This notion that the Word of God, as it is heard by the sinner-declared-saint, binds the conscience to it, serves as a warning to Lutherans not to dismiss summarily the person who makes such a claim. We are neither pope nor emperor but fellow believers to one another. This means that we cannot simply assert one interpretation of Scripture over another but must always respect the conscience of others with whom we may disagree."[13]

The interplay between community and the individual is necessary. The church is never perfect, but always reforming. We don't expect or claim infallibility either for the community or the individual. Both are *simul justus et peccator.*

In 2005 I had the privilege of spending three days with ELCA and LCMS military chaplains. Several have served in Iraq and Afghanistan. Some were activated reserves who had to leave congregations. All were experiencing the incredible challenges of ministry in a time of war.

The topic of the conference was "Just War/Just Peace." Together with a Lutheran ethicist and a Muslim who has written on *jihad* and terrorism, we struggled with questions of conscience in the context of modern warfare. We reexamined the just war tradition as Luther received and interpreted it. We reflected upon the Lutheran Confessions and the writings of Luther on civil authority, conscience, military service. We discussed the changes in how wars are fought and for what purpose. Some of us argued that the most consistent Lutheran position is one that recognizes selective conscientious objection, yet such a position is difficult to hold given current military standards.

In the midst of our lively probing questions and our deeply held convictions, we would stop to hear God's word, worship, sing, and pray. I believe we were being the body of Christ engaged in moral deliberation.

In the body of Christ, our unity is not based on an agreement on every issue, but on a shared faith in the gospel. Before we seek to grow together or fear growing apart, we are bold to confess who and whose we are. As Dietrich Bonhoeffer reminds us, the unity of the church as the body of Christ is not a goal to be attained, but a fact to be recognized. According to this image, the mission of the church is not to achieve unity but to act as the unified body it is. We do so not only for the sake of unity, but so the world might believe (John 17). By the power of the Holy Spirit, we seek to grow together as the community we already are in Christ for the sake of God's mission in the world.

We do the ongoing work of interpreting the Bible as brothers and sisters in Christ by virtue of our baptism. Through baptism we are incorporated into the church, the body of Christ, in which not everything goes, but everyone is welcome.

William Sloane Coffin in *Credo* reminds us: "So what the Christian community needs to do above all else is to raise up men and women of thought and of conscience, adventuresome, imaginative people capable of both joy and suffering. And most of all they must be people of courage so that when the day goes hard and cowards steal from the field, like Luther, they will be able to say, 'My conscience is captive to the Word of God . . . to go against conscience is neither right nor safe. Here I stand. I can do no other. God help me.' Our faith should quell our fears, never our courage."[14]

To live with faith and courage in unsettling times, we need to keep our eyes on the one who calls us, our ears open to his word, as Dietrich Bonhoeffer writes: "Where will the call to discipleship lead those who follow it? What decisions and painful separations will it entail? We must take this question to him who alone knows the answer. Only Jesus Christ, who bids us follow him, knows where the path will lead. But we know that it will be a path full of mercy beyond measure. Discipleship is joy."[15]

Questions for Reflection and Discussion

1. How do you react to talk of commands and obedience in reference to God?

2. Do you agree that we in the Lutheran church hesitate speaking about the commands of Jesus in the Bible? Why or why not?

3. What does it mean to you to confess with the early Christians: "Jesus is Lord"?

4. How do you understand the difference between inviting Jesus into your life and having Jesus invite you into his?

5. How might these commands of God in the Bible be "words of freedom" for you?

> "What does the Lord require of you but to do justice, to love kindness, and to walk humbly with your God?" (Micah 6:8).
> "I give you a new commandment, that you love one another" (John 13:34).
> "Do not be conformed to this world, but be transformed by the renewing of your minds" (Romans 12:2).
> "Bear one another's burdens, and in this way you will fulfill the law of Christ" (Galatians 6:2).

"Love your enemies and pray for those who persecute you, so that you may be children of your Father in heaven" (Matthew 5:44-45).

"Go therefore and make disciples of all nations, baptizing them in the name of the Father and of the Son and of the Holy Spirit, and teaching them to obey everything that I have commanded you" (Matthew 28:19-20).

6. Thinking of the concept of ethical triaging, what are some ethical or moral issues you think Christians most need to address together? Why do you choose those issues?

7. How can we in the church wrestle with the difficult issues without tearing ourselves apart?

8. What did you find most interesting or helpful in this chapter?

9. What questions do you have after studying this chapter?

4. Discerning Our Way in the World

We have been thinking together about a Christian life trusting in the promises of God, wrestling with Jesus' probing questions, and obeying God's clear commands.

Where is such a life to be lived? The answer is that we are called and sent *into the world* to live this life as followers of Jesus and members of the body of Christ. We pray in the Lord's Prayer for God's kingdom to come and God's will be done *on earth,* as it is already being done in heaven. We have the promise of Jesus, "You will receive power when the Holy Spirit has come upon you" and his command, "You will be my witnesses" (Acts 1:8).

When I consider how the Bible describes the world and the relationship of the believer to the world, I believe that our way of being in the world involves at least three very different responses:

- at times we are sent to be <u>actively engaged</u> in the world;
- at other times, we are called to <u>acts of resistance</u> in the world;

- at the same time we are to <u>remain detached</u> from the world.

Engaged in the World

The opening verse of Genesis 1 can be translated, "When God *began* to create . . ." God is still in the process of creating, loving, and reconciling the world. In perhaps the best-known verse of the Bible we read that "God so loved *the world* that he gave his only begotten son" (John 3:16). If we believe that the world is the object of God's love, then as people of God we will be engaged in the world. In so doing, we are keeping the promise made in the baptismal covenant: "to proclaim the good news of God in Christ, through word and deed," "to serve all people following the example of Christ" and "to strive for justice and peace in all the earth."[1]

Darrell Jodock has said: "If we are to revitalize Christian discipleship or vocation in the world, we need to begin by rebuilding a theological foundation to support it. And my suggestion is that the best theological base is Luther's concept of God active in the world. For Luther, God is at work everywhere—in families, in the workplace, in the public life of the community, in international affairs—everywhere. This ubiquitous activity does not mean, of course, that God causes everything to happen that happens—indeed, much of what happens does not at all please God and is contrary to God's purposes—but God is nonetheless at work, amid the ambiguity and the conflict, to enhance human dignity and to advance the cause of justice."[2]

To share in God's work of "enhancing human dignity and advancing the cause of justice," we can engage in several actions, among them communal lamenting, seeking signs of God at work, and serving through our varying vocations.

Communal lamenting. One place to begin is with communal lament, listening to the pain of our community and our world and giving it voice. Communal lament is born out of engagement with the world as it is and a vision of the world as God intends it to be.

I will never forget one of those significant—dare I say life-changing—encounters that occurred when I was in high school. In my senior year our "Modern Problems" teacher took us to Augsburg College to hear a lecture by Louis Lomax, author of *The Negro Revolt.* It was absolutely jarring to hear firsthand, persuasively, passionately, and prophetically the injustice of racial discrimination and segregation in America. I thought, "It cannot be. It must not be. If so, we must change it."

Yet my lament was deep inside—not yet publicly shared—until college and seminary and the opportunity for public engagement in the movement for civil rights. After my sophomore year of college, many college campuses sent teams of eight to be immersed in the city in a program called "Listening Witness." The first goal was not to do something, but to listen to those in poverty and to congregations in changing neighborhoods. We were to listen with questions like these in mind: "Where is the voice of God? What does it mean to be a witness to God's presence in this conflicted, chaotic situation?" Such compassionate listening might lead us to feel the distress of the people.

Professor Cynthia Moe-Lobeda in her exceptional book *Public Church: For the Life of the World* writes: "Communal lament . . . is the assembly crying out in distress to the God in whom it trusts. . . . Deep and sincere communal lament . . . names problems, seeks justice, and hopes for God's deliverance. Lament . . . forms people; it requires them to give name and words to suffering." Such lament may move us to ask, 'Where is God in this situation?'"[3]

Seeking signs of God at work. Moe-Lobeda asks, "Amidst the complexity and moral ambiguity of life, how are we to discern what God is doing in any given situation, and how might we most faithfully give social form to God's work? In both interpersonal and international venues how are we to discern what God is doing, so that we may align ourselves with it? Lutheran theology offers invaluable clues. It assures us that human beings cannot know with certainty what God is doing in the world, yet, paradoxically and in the face of uncertainty, we are to act in accord with God's mission and activity as we understand it through faithful discernment."[4]

She adds: "The heart of discernment is to hold 'what is' and 'what could be' in the light of the life-giving, life-saving, life-sustaining mystery of God's ongoing work toward the redemption and flourishing of creation.... Where visions of life's realities are obscured by illusions, a task of Christian discernment is to see differently so that we might live differently. Where dominant forces distort historical realities by describing them falsely, Christian discernment must re-see and then re-describe the world."[5]

Bonhoeffer reminds us that as Lutherans, embracing a theology of the cross is central to our seeing, which means that seeing from below, from the perspective of the outcasts, the suspects, the maltreated, the powerless, the oppressed, the reviled—in short, from the perspective of those who suffer—is "an experience of incomparable worth."[6]

On a recent trip to West Africa the lament of Jeremiah took on new meaning for me. The prophet mourned for the people: "My joy is gone, grief is upon me, my heart is sick. . . . For the hurt of my poor people I am hurt, I mourn and dismay has taken hold of me. Is there no balm in Gilead? Is there no physician there? Why then has the health of my poor people not been restored? O that my head were a spring of water, and my eyes a fountain of tears, so that I might weep day and night for the slain of my poor people" (Jeremiah 8:18, 21, 22; 9:1).

Years of civil war in Liberia and Sierra Leone have come to an end. Three times during the war Phebe Hospital in Liberia came under attack. Each time the medical staff and nursing students had to flee to villages miles away, yet they never ceased to be a healing balm. Just nine months after the hospital was ransacked, we joined in a service of rededication. Thanks to the resiliency of the Liberian people, the leadership of the Lutheran Church in Liberia, the generosity of the Norwegian people, volunteers from the United States and other nations, the accompaniment of the ELCA, the hospital is again offering much needed medical care. There is a physician in Phebe! Signs of the healing presence and power of the Holy Spirit break into the midst of war and destruction. In both Liberia and Sierra Leone, Christians join with Muslims not demanding retaliation but seeking reconciliation. What a powerful witness to God's healing mercy!

Serving through our varying vocations. In Martin Luther's concept of vocation, we find deep, practical guidance on how to be engaged in the world. As Luther taught, we are engaged according to our callings in life: through our paid work, in the family, in the community, in political life. In each of these places, we become the means by which God's blessings reach others.

The call to live out our faith in public witness in the world is and must be made compelling. It belongs to the vocation of the baptized. We make that clear when in the Lutheran rite of confirmation we ask those affirming their baptism, "Do you intend to continue in the covenant God made with you in Holy Baptism?" Then we go on to describe what life in God's baptismal grace—God's covenantal community—means: "to live among God's faithful people, to hear this Word and share in his supper, to proclaim the good news of God in Christ through word and deed, to serve all people, following the example of our Lord Jesus, and to strive for justice and peace in all the earth."[7]

In discerning how we as individuals carry out that service and strive for peace and justice we will be guided by the gifts God has given us and the situations in which God has placed us. Discerning those gifts and our life situations is, for most of us, a lifelong process.

Our oldest daughter spent her first two years at a prestigious women's college. As an adopted biracial high-school student, she was very clear that she did not want to attend a predominantly white,

European-American college. The woman's college was wonderful for her, immersing her in an Afrocentric, womanist curriculum and environment. After her sophomore year, with her belongings still on campus, she came home for the summer. One evening with tears in her eyes, she announced, "I want to transfer to Augsburg College." Her reasons were thoughtful and decisive. She did transfer, she graduated, and now is a high school math teacher and instructor in the Augsburg Weekend College.

One evening she reflected on that decision: "My first two years I was being pushed to find a career in which the primary goal was to be successful. Augsburg College helped me find my calling, where I could use my gifts and make a difference in the lives of others. I never would have been a math teacher if I would not have transferred. I am so glad I did, because teaching is my calling." She continues to pursue that calling as well as her other callings as a mother, daughter, sister, and member of a Christian congregation.

Serving God in our various callings in life may bring us meaning and joy, but at times also frustration and opposition. Believing in God's promises, we will not be easily discouraged or defeated as we carry out our service of striving for justice and peace. By faith we live out Paul's declaration: "Therefore, since it is by God's mercy that we are engaged in this ministry, we do not lose heart.... We are afflicted in every way, but not crushed; perplexed, but not driven to despair; persecuted, but not forsaken; struck down, but not destroyed, always carrying in the body the death of Jesus, so that the life of Jesus may also be made visible in our bodies" (2 Corinthians 4:1-10).

"Not losing heart" is, I believe, a call to evangelical persistence. We believe that it is by God's mercy that we are engaged in this ministry, and we trust Jesus' promise "Remember, I am with you always, to the end of the age" (Matthew 28:20). So we persevere proclaiming the gospel, serving our neighbor, caring for the creation, and living out our baptismal identity in our varied callings.

Evangelical persistence is a mark of many faithful and courageous people who are experiencing the great changes in rural America. Two recent gatherings of laity and clergy living in the open country and small towns attest to this reality. From the outside we see aging communities, diminishing numbers of people engaged in farming, consolidating schools, businesses and churches closing. In the midst of those realities I witnessed amazing evangelical perseverance.

Representatives of seven congregations in Iowa formed a task force that met monthly for years. The driving question was not, "How do we keep our individual congregations open?" but "What gifts do we bring to God's mission in our changing communities?" One Sunday, members of the seven congregations joined in a festival service of worship as One in Christ Lutheran Parish was born, the third largest congregation in the Northeastern Iowa Synod. A turning point in the planning process, according to one participant, was when "we decided we seven congregations must believe—all the way down to our guts—that we exist for the sake of those not here. Christ's gaze is always outward, and Christ's church must go in the same direction."

Evangelical Resistance

This is God's world, but it is a fallen world in which Christians struggle against the powers that are opposed to God and the kingdom of God. Therefore sometimes our stance in the world is one of evangelical resistance or what the late Lutheran leader Will Herzfeld called "evangelical defiance."

The focus of our resistance is "the powers" described in the letter to the Ephesians: "For our struggle is not against enemies of blood and flesh, but against the rulers, against the authorities, against the cosmic powers of this present darkness, against the spiritual forces of evil in the heavenly places" (Ephesians 6:12).

Although the world is being created and reconciled by God, it is also where the devil prowls, seeking someone to devour (1 Peter 5:8). As communities of discernment, we learn to know the signs of the presence of evil, to be alert to the demonic forces that seek to separate the creation and God's people from life in God's presence and promises. According to God's command, we are to "Resist [the devil], steadfast in your faith, for you know that your brothers and sisters in all the world are undergoing the same kinds of suffering." And we have God's promise: "Resist the devil, and he will flee from you" (James 4:7).

We ask at the beginning of the baptismal service: "Do you renounce the forces of evil, the devil, and the devil's empty promises?" We are called on to renounce the forces that defy God and that rebel against God and draw us away from God.[8]

Seminary professor Craig Nessan has written: "Luther understood God to be engaged in fierce competition with Satan for control over the world. In the contest, God employs two distinct 'strategies,' a left-hand strategy of temporal governance and a right-hand strategy of spiritual governance. Traditionally these two strategies have been referred to as the two 'kingdoms.' In the left-hand strategy, God seeks to provide good and just order in the world through government, labor, and family life. In this strategy, God works through the structures of the world. In the right-hand strategy, God works through the theological use of the law, the gospel of Jesus Christ, and the freedom of the gospel. The gospel sets us free from sin, death, and the power of Satan and free for serving the needs of the neighbor."[9]

In participating in these two "strategies" of God, we must resist the seductive power of the world, the national and global society in which we live.

This is no easy task. Cynthia Moe-Lobeda has written: "Faith-based resistance is fraught with ambiguity and born of repentance and humility. It entails taking a stand in a world where moral certainty often is impossible and human efforts toward the good are intermingled with sin, where self-righteousness rears its head in the midst of self-giving actions and the pull to equate one's course to the will of God is almost magnetic. Thus Christian resistance, and in particular, Lutheran Christian resistance, is housed in a conviction that the hopes of the resisters, the alternatives toward which they point or the policies they promote are not the gospel of Christ or the reign of God. These efforts and visions—honest and noble as they may be—are fallible human attempts to know and approximate ways of living consistent with the God revealed in Jesus Christ. In emphasizing this conviction, even insisting upon it, Lutheran Christian resistance offers invaluable service to the broader public."[10]

Some acts of resistance born out of consensus shaped by the word of God draw public attention. Others are carried out quietly, faithfully, courageously. The family that resolves not to orient their entire day around patterns of consumptive, rat-race living but turn off the television, and gather nightly at the table for prayer, conversation, and food just may be engaged in an act of resistance. The same is true for the farmer who seeks to make decisions about crops, fertilizers, and pesticides that will increase yield yet not destroy the environment. The high school student who is willing to confront friends for their condescending attitude toward their new Muslim classmate who has immigrated from Somalia is practicing courage and faithfulness.

Detachment from the World

This is God's world, and yet "here we have no lasting city, but we are looking for the city that is to come" (Hebrews 13:14).

This world is not finally our home; we are sojourners passing through. As sojourners we are guided by Paul's admonition: "Be not conformed to this world, but be transformed by the renewing of your mind" (Romans 12:2). We practice this kind of countercultural life by offering ourselves as living sacrifices, by seeing the world "other-wise," by remaining detached from the world.

Detachment is not the same as withdrawal, which is becoming permanently disengaged by hiding behind self-constructed walls in the equivalent of cultural or religious gated communities. Detachment means not clinging to the world or our place in the world, nor our power or standing. Detachment means not building our own kingdoms here on earth. Detachment often requires solitude and silence. In the Gospels we read of times when Jesus invited his disciples away from the clamoring and needy crowds to come and be alone with him. We too need to disengage for a time, to be consciously in God's presence, to regain perspective, to pray for discernment and strength to move back out in the world with new vision, courage, and strength.

Even while we are engaged in the world, we remain detached by remembering that the results of our engagement are not up to us. We need evangelical patience and persistence and hope as we wait for God to bring in the kingdom. We will never see the reign of God fully come in our time, in our human history. Reinhold Niebuhr wrote, "Nothing that is worth doing can be achieved in our lifetime; therefore, we must be saved by hope. Nothing which is true, or beautiful, or good makes complete sense in any immediate context of history; therefore, we must be saved by faith. Nothing we do, however virtuous, could be accomplished alone; therefore, we must be saved by love. No virtuous act is quite as virtuous from the standpoint of our friend or foe as it is from our own standpoint; therefore, we must be saved by the final form of love, which is forgiveness."[11]

Often I have stood in front of a group and pleaded, "Don't just stand there, do something!" It may be that we also need to do the opposite— "Don't just do something, stand there." The invitation to stand in the presence of God's faithful promises and with those who are suffering may become the occasion for faithful, patient waiting. It may become the occasion for courageous, prophetic speech. The Apostle James writes, "Be patient, therefore, beloved, until the coming of the Lord. The farmer waits for the precious crop from the earth, being patient with it until it receives the early and the late rains. . . . As an example of suffering and patience, beloved, take the prophets who spoke in the name of the Lord" (5: 7, 10).

This spirit of waiting is expressed especially in the season of Advent, a time of waiting for God. In an article titled "I Am an Advent Christian," Ron Klug wrote: "Waiting calls me back to standing on God's promises: 'Beloved, we are God's children now; what we will be has not yet been revealed. What we do know is this: when he is revealed, we will be like him, for we shall see him as he is' (1 John 3:2-3). 'But in accordance with his promise, we wait for new heavens and a new earth, where righteousness is at home' (2 Peter 3:13).

"As an Advent Christian, I am sustained by these promises. I can accept my exile and the experience of suffering in the world. I don't have to pretend that this life is all there is. I can live with my longings; I don't need to deny them. I can be mindful of the reality around me. I can sing of the reality to come. And I can practice waiting."[12]

I will never forget visiting a camp for refugees in Liberia. These Liberians had been displaced when their homes and villages were destroyed by warring rebels. More than twenty thousand people had constructed small temporary shelters. With assistance from staff of the Lutheran World Federation World Service and food aid from the United Nations, they began to organize themselves into a community. Yet in their speech and eyes was the absolute resolve to return home to reconstruct their lives there. Many who spoke with us revealed that their hope was in God's faithfulness. God's promise spoken through the prophet Isaiah was also spoken to them: "Do not fear, for I have redeemed you; I have called you by name, you are mine. When you pass through the waters, I will be with you; and through the rivers, they shall not overwhelm you. . . . For I am the Lord your God, the Holy One of Israel, your Savior" (Isaiah 43:1-3).

Discerning the Way

How are we to be engaged in the world? When and how are we asked to resist and confront evil? How do we remain detached from the world? These questions pose a daunting task of discernment and living that requires an active life in community. Together and as individuals we need to hear and study the Bible so we have a more full understanding of these three ways of being faithful in the world. We also need a prayerful approach to every day: "God, grant me the ability to know where you are calling me to be engaged. How can I be bold to cast out evil in your name? How can I stay detached?"

To begin to answer those questions, I need to be in a community of discernment. My image of congregational life is of an assembly that gathers weekly around the means of grace to sing God's praises, to make intercession, to hear God's word of promise, to be challenged by Jesus' probing questions, and to be a community of prayerful discernment around the question: "How are we going to live all this out in the coming week?" We need to ask this as individuals and as a community.

If I were back in the parish, I as pastor would gather with the faithful, and we would read a text concerning one of these ways of being in the world, and I would ask, How did it go this week? Where were you given opportunities to live out your faith? Where did you confront evil? And where this week were you able to be detached?"

Then we would talk about the week ahead. What does your week look like in the light of these three ways of being in the world: engagement, resistance, detachment? We would pray for one another and for our life together in the world. And we would send one another out on our individual and communal ways.

In the offertory prayer of our liturgy we pray: "Blessed are you, O Lord our God, maker of all things. Through your goodness you have blessed us with these gifts. With them we offer ourselves to your service and dedicate our lives to the care and redemption of all that you have made, for the sake of him who gave himself for us, Jesus Christ our Lord."[13]

Drawing on the thought of Dietrich Bonhoeffer, Lisa E. Dahill emphasizes that discernment is part of the Christian's life with and in Christ: "Discernment for Christians isn't only about making wise decisions in accord with God's will—it's about love, living in love with Jesus Christ. Throughout his life Bonhoeffer reminds us that the point of discipleship, or learning to follow Jesus wherever he leads, isn't any predetermined program or agenda. The point is solely and only Jesus himself: our hearts' intimacy with this One who is love incarnate for us and for all, and with those in whom he is present today."[14]

The Communal Way in the World

The three ways of being in the world—engagement, resistance, and detachment—apply to individual Christians, but also to the communal experience of the church engaged in the world in acts of mercy and the pursuit of justice and peace. Where are we struggling for peace? Where are we challenging the political powers? Where is the church called to resist evil? How does the church remain detached from this world?

Rather than pitting ourselves against one another, in congregations or denominations, we need to bring these concerns into a common conversation. We do this not as conservatives or liberals, Republicans or Democrats, but as brothers and sisters, children of one God who respect and love one another.

We need one another to do all this, and we also need those now outside the boundaries of the church, just as they need us. We can look for opportunities to invite others to hear the promises of God. We can invite them to bring their questions and to join with us in searching for answers. We can expose them to the probing questions of Jesus. We can challenge them to join us in doing the faith, in obeying the commands of Jesus. And we can ask for their help as we discern our way in the world—in engagement, in resistance, in detachment.

One way this is happening in many parts of the United States is through what is referred to as "congregation-based organizing." In Milwaukee, for example, an interfaith network called MICAH, Milwaukee Innercity Congregations Allied for Hope, is comprised of thirty-seven Christian, Islamic, and Jewish congregations who have joined together to work for justice in Milwaukee's inner city. Among their achievements has been a "banking campaign" in which they persuaded seventeen lending institutions to set aside $500,000,000 for loans to first-time home buyers in central city Milwaukee. By setting less rigid lending policies, the lending institutions have allowed about seventy-five families a month for seven to eight years to buy their own homes. In a another major push, the congregations working together have succeeded in getting the Milwaukee Public Schools to raise the number of SAGE schools (classrooms of less than fifteen students) from ten to sixty-seven. Other congregation-based organizing efforts have been directed at encouraging treatment rather than prison for drug offenders, developing affordable housing, and safeguarding the civil rights of immigrants.

To do this kind of inviting—of other Christians, members of other religions, spiritual seekers, other citizens—we need what John H.

Thomas calls "bridge builders." Bridge builders, he says, "don't impose uniformity; they seek to enable different communities to become a diverse community."[15]

As we invite others to join us as people of the promise, we remember that God's promises are never static. Theologian Peter Hawkins has referred to the "improvisational God," the God who is always doing a new thing. God is always finding new ways to be faithful to God's promises. Who could ever imagine that God would have become flesh and live among us?

To help us recognize the new things God is doing, we need seers, people of startling vision. According to John H. Thomas, these include poets and artists. Thomas says, "Poets and liturgists are today's evangelists who enable us to sense the improvisational God revealed in Jesus Christ, and lure us into the company of those who are no longer satisfied with consuming or with living as competitive strangers to one another."[16]

Guided by the prophets and poets and bridge builders among us, we discern our way in this world, sometimes engaging the world as cocreators with God, sometimes resisting the world in acts of evangelical defiance, and simultaneously remaining detached from the world. Living in the creative tension of these ways of being in the world, we as individuals and as the church are being faithful to the God who is always and eternally being faithful to us. We live in the words of St. Paul; "Keep alert, stand firm in your faith, be courageous, be strong. Let all that you do be done in love" (1 Corinthians 16:13-14).

Questions for Reflection and Discussion

1. What do you see God doing in the world? How do you know? What does it mean to view the world "from below," from those on the margins?

2. Respond to this statement of Cynthia Moe-Lobeda: "Human beings cannot know with certainty what God is doing in the world, yet, paradoxically, and in the face of uncertainty, we are to act in accord with God's mission and activity as we understand it through faithful discernment."

3. In what ways are you actively engaged in the world, as a cocreator with God?

4. Where do you see the devil or the forces of evil active in the world? What are you doing to resist those forces?

5. Why is it important for us to remain detached from the world, while being engaged and in resistance? How might we do that?

6. How does your congregation help you discern your way in the world—through engagement, resistance, or detachment? What additional help might it offer?

7. What do you think of the concept of "the improvisational God"?

8. What did you find most interesting or helpful in this chapter?

9. What questions do you have as a result of studying this chapter?

For further information on congregation-based organizing, see Dennis A. Jacobsen, *Doing Justice: Congregational and Community Organizing* (Minneapolis: Fortress Press, 2001).

Web sites: www.gamaliel. org
www.isaiah.org

NOTES

Chapter 1. Trusting God's Promises
1. *Lutheran Book of Worship (LBW)* (Minneapolis: Augsburg Fortress, 1978), 77.
2. *LBW*, 201.
3. "Children of the Heav'nly Father," *LBW*, 474, st. 1, 3.
4. *LBW*, 201.
5. *Occasional Services* (Minneapolis: Augsburg Publishing House, and Philadelphia: Board of Publication, Lutheran Church in America, 1982), 226.

Chapter 2. Pondering Jesus' Probing Questions
1. Joseph Sittler, *Gravity and Grace* (Minneapolis: Augsburg Fortress, 2005), 3.
2. Jonathan Strandjord, from address for opening convocation at the Lutheran Theological Seminary at Philadelphia (September 3, 2002). Used by permission.
3. Dietrich Bonhoeffer, *Life Together* (Minneapolis: Fortress Press, 1996), 98.
4. John H. Thomas, from "Pontiff, Prophet, Poet," address to the Annual Consultation of the United Church of Christ (February 20, 2002). Used by permission.
5. H. George Anderson, *A Good Time to Be the Church* (Minneapolis: Augsburg Books, 1997), 48.
6. Ibid., 53.

Chapter 3. Obeying Jesus' Unsettling Commands
1. Mark Allan Powell, *Loving Jesus* (Minneapolis: Fortress Press, 2004) 179.
2. Mark Kolden, *The Christian's Calling in the World* (St. Paul: Centered Life, 2002), 7-8.
3. *A Contemporary Translation of Luther's Small Catechism* (Minneapolis: Augsburg Fortress, 1994), 17.
4. James D. Whitehead and Evelyn Eaton Whitehead, *Shadows of the Heart: A Spirituality of the Negative Emotions* (New York: Crossroad, 1994), 7.
5. Martin Luther, "The Freedom of the Christian" in *Martin Luther's Basic Theological Writings* (Minneapolis: Fortress Press, 1989), 596.
6. Darrell Jodock, from an address given to the Convocation of Bishops and Teaching Theologians, January 10, 2005. Used by permission.

7. Munib Younan, *Witnessing for Peace* (Minneapolis: Fortress Press, 2003), 42.

8. Lisa E. Dahill, "We Do Not Know What to Do, But Our Eyes Are on Thee," *The Lutheran* (April 2005), 27-28.

9. Sittler, 67.

10. Mark Allan Powell, "Binding and Loosing: Asserting the Moral Authority of Scripture in Light of a Matthean Paradigm" *Ex Auditu* 19 (2003), 81-82.

11. Dahill, 28.

12. Translation of quote in *Deutsche Reichstagsakten* (Göttingen: Vandenhoeck and Ruprecht, 1962), 550.

13. Timothy Wengert from a lecture titled, "Reflections on the Bound Conscience in Lutheran Theology."

14. William Sloane Coffin, *Credo* (Louisville: Westminster John Knox, 2003), 70-71.

15. Dietrich Bonhoeffer, *Discipleship* (Minneapolis: Fortress Press, 2003), 40.

Chapter 4. Discerning Our Way in the World

1. *LBW*, 201.

2. Darrell Jodock, from an address given to the Convocation of Bishops and Teaching Theologians, January 10, 2005. Used by permission.

3. Cynthia Moe-Lobeda, *Public Church: For the Life of the World* (Minneapolis: Augsburg Fortress, 2004), 68.

4. Ibid., 64.

5. Ibid., 65-66.

6. Quoted in Moe-Lobeda, 66.

7. *LBW*, 201.

8. Ibid.

9. Craig L. Nessan, "Social Ministry and Evangelism," in Norma Cook Everist and Craig L. Nessan, eds., *Forming an Evangelizing People: Perspectives and Questions for Use in the Church* (Dubuque, Iowa.: Wartburg Theological Seminary, 2005), 14.

10. Moe-Lobeda, 70.

11. Reinhold Niebuhr, *Irony of American History*. (New York: Scribners, 1952), 63.

12. Ron Klug, "I Am an Advent Christian," *The Lutheran* (December, 1999), 12.

13. *LBW*, 88.

14. Dahill, 28.

15. John H. Thomas, from "Pontiff, Prophet, Poet," address to the Annual Consultation of the United Church of Christ, February 20, 2002. Used by permission.

16. Thomas, "Pontiff, Prophet, Poet."

Other Resources from Augsburg Fortress

Faithful yet Changing by Bishop Mark S. Hanson
88 pages, 0-8066-4474-5

Bishop Hanson issues an urgent call to mission
marked by witnessing, worshiping, engaging,
equipping, inviting, connecting, changing, and
praying.

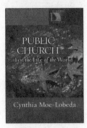

Public Church by Cynthia Moe-Lobeda
112 pages, 0-8066-4987-9

The ELCA professes to be a public church
constituted by God for its public vocation.
Moe-Lobeda explores what it means for the
ELCA to play a role in public life today.

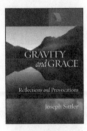

Gravity and Grace by Joseph Sittler
128 pages, 0-8066-5173-3

This newly revised edition provides insights
from one of the leading Lutheran theologians
of the twentieth century. Study questions are
provided to encourage group discussion.

Loving Jesus by Mark Allan Powell
208 pages, 0-8006-3676-7

In this biblical spirituality for today, Powell's
plea is for Christians to revisit their faith not by
blazing in religious enthusiasm but by harbor-
ing a steadier flame and deeper commitment.

Available wherever books are sold.